Life Starts Now

Mark Boer

Life Starts Now

Mark Boer

Life Starts Now
Copyright ©2020 by Mark Boer
ISBN 979-8-218-11092-5

Requests for information should be addressed to: Mark Boer
Life Church 3225 E. Commercial Ct, Meridian, ID 83642

Unless otherwise indicated, Scripture taken from the New King James Version®. Copyright © 1982 by Thomas Nelson. Used by permission. All rights reserved.

Other Scripture versions cited are as follows:

Amplified Bible, Classic Edition (AMPC)

"Scripture quotations taken from the Amplified® Bible (AMPC), Copyright © 1954, 1958, 1962, 1964, 1965, 1987 by The Lockman Foundation Used by permission. www.Lockman.org"

King James Version (KJV)

KJV is public domain in the United States.

All rights reserved. No part of this publication may be reproduced, stored in a retrieval system or transmitted in any form or by any means—electronic, mechanical, photocopy, recording or any other—except for brief quotations in printed reviews, without the prior permission of the publisher.

Published by: Mark Boer
              3225 E. Commercial Ct
              Meridian, ID 83642

Printed in the United States of America.

2020

Contents

Chapter One: What Just Happened?   7

Chapter Two: New Creation   15

Chapter Three: New Habits   23

Chapter Four: New Relationships   30

Chapter Five: New Way of Living   38

Chapter Six: What's Next   47

Conclusion   60

Glossary: Common Christian Words   61

Chapter 1
What Just Happened?

So, you just prayed and received Jesus as your Lord and Savior. Are you "spinning" a bit inside? Are you trying to wrap your mind around what just happened? Maybe you took much time to contemplate this decision and are fully aware of its magnitude, or maybe you simply responded in the moment to what seemed like the right thing to do deep down inside. Either way, congratulations!

You made it. You're in. In the family of God, that is. You are no longer on the outside looking in but have fully received the most important gift available to a human being—salvation. Think about it. You are saved! You will not go to hell. One day, you will experience the incomprehensible glories of heaven. This really just happened. Let it sink in. Maybe take a selfie. This is a day to celebrate!

LIFE STARTS NOW

This experience is referred to by several different terms in the Bible. You could say it several different ways and they would all be correct:

- I got saved. (Romans 10:9)
- I was born-again. (John 3:3)
- I became a new creation in Christ. (2 Corinthians 5:17)
- I repented. (Acts 3:19)
- I experienced regeneration. (Titus 3:5)
- I believed in Jesus. (1 John 5:1)
- I received Jesus. (Colossians 2:6; John 1:12)

Whichever word you use, it is a very big deal. For the rest of your days on earth and forever, you will look back to this point as being the defining moment of your life. Also, you will continue to learn about the depth of this event. It is an encounter with God Almighty that is very far-reaching. It affects both the "here and now" and eternity.

Let's take a moment to review the prayer you just prayed. (If you are reading this and have not yet received Jesus, you could pray this right now.) It's not that there is one specific prayer that has to have these exact phrases but rather one that contains the gist of what it takes to receive salvation. You probably said something like this:

Dear God in heaven,
I repent of my sins and turn my life to You.
I believe in Jesus. He died for me on the cross, paying for all my sins.
He was raised from the dead and is alive today.
I receive Him now as my Savior. I confess that Jesus is Lord.
I give all my heart and all my life to You.
I receive your forgiveness, love and eternal life.
According to Your word, I am now saved. I have been born-again.
I am in Your family.
I'll never be the same again.
In Jesus' name, I pray. Amen!

This is not a prayer that one should pray over and over again. It is a one-time commitment to God and the reception of the gift of eternal life. If you prayed it, know that God heard you and you are now saved. Your sins are gone, forever forgiven. Psalms 103:12 reads, "As far as the east is from the west, *So* far has He removed our transgressions from us."

To begin understanding the salvation experience, let's break down this prayer and its vital components. This is what you did when you prayed. This is what happened to you.

1. You repented of sin.

   > Repent therefore and be converted,
   > that your sins may be blotted out,
   > so that times of refreshing may
   > come from the presence of the
   > Lord. (Acts 3:19)

   This is an act of turning from one way of thinking and living to another way. It is renouncing a life of sin, selfishness and worldliness and then embracing God's way of doing things. It is saying to God that you are turning your back on your old life and starting over with Him.

2. You believed in Jesus and what He did for you.

That if you confess with your mouth the Lord Jesus and believe in your heart that God has raised Him from the dead, you will be saved. (Romans 10:9)

Who [Jesus] Himself bore our sins in His own body on the tree, that we, having died to sins, might live for righteousness—by whose stripes you were healed.
(1 Peter 2:24)

Believing that Jesus died for and fully paid the price owed for all your sins is a vital part of being saved. Religion doesn't save people. Good works don't save people. The fact is, there is nothing we could ever do to save ourselves from the consequences of sin. However, God did for us what we could never do for ourselves. He solved the sin problem. He took all of our sin and placed it on His Son Jesus. He suffered tremendously and died. He paid the full price for our salvation. We could say that He paid our bill; He served our sentence; He satisfied the requirements of the high court of heaven so we could walk free.

3. You received the Savior and confessed His lordship.

As noted in Romans 10:9 (found above), part of our salvation is the confession that Jesus is Lord. When we do this, we are simply saying that He is now the supreme authority in our lives. He is being given the right to call the shots. We are removing Satan, sin, and even ourselves from the throne of our hearts and humbly giving that place to Jesus. You can see that a proud person cannot be saved. This is not about us proclaiming our ways and demanding that God accept us but rather a submission to God's ways and a willingness to change. This is both a one-time event and a continual way of living. Any time a true Christian realizes that God wants him to do something different, that believer makes the necessary adjustments in order to align with God's plan.

I would encourage you to not see this as a binding obligation but rather a liberating relationship with a God who loves you. This is a good thing. To have a relationship with God and walk in truth will produce a greater joy than can ever be known any other way.

Salvation, once received, becomes a current possession. We don't get eternal life when we die. We get it the moment we receive Jesus. The apostle John said it this way: "These things I have written to you who believe in the name of the Son of God, that you may know that you have eternal life, and that you may *continue to* believe in the name of the Son of God." 1 John 5:13

So then, there is no need to be born-again again. Failure does not mean that one loses his salvation. Sometimes people ask, "What if I sin and then die before I get a chance to confess it before God?" You didn't get saved by confessing your sins. **You got saved by confessing the Lordship of Jesus.** Therefore, the absence of officially "handling" with sufficient remorse each and every sin committed (those of thought, word and deed) and even the failure to do something that ought to have been done (sin of omission) has no bearing on your eternal destination. You are still a child of God.

Should we repent (turn from) wrongdoing continually? Of course. Should we strive to live holy, separated lives? For sure. Just do this from a position of knowing that you are already a part of God's eternal kingdom and family. Don't live as if you have to repeatedly regain your salvation.

Chapter 2
New Creation

Therefore, if anyone *is* in Christ, *he is* a new creation; old things have passed away; behold, all things have become new. (2 Corinthians 5:17)

A person who receives salvation is new. Therefore, you are no longer the same person you used to be. You may be quick to say "Amen!" to this because you feel different than you did before, or you may be wondering what is really different. This is where we need a little lesson in the makeup of a human being. You see, if we only think of ourselves in regard to our physical being, we will not be able to understand much of the Bible or spiritual realities and will gage our spiritual condition and standing with God on how we feel at any given time. The truth is that we are three-part beings: spirit, soul, and body. The Word of God declares:

LIFE STARTS NOW

Now may the God of peace Himself sanctify you completely; and may your whole spirit, soul, and body be preserved blameless at the coming of our Lord Jesus Christ. (1 Thessalonians 5:23)

The spirit is the eternal part of you: the part that will live on after your body dies. It is the part that contacts the spirit world and God, who is a Spirit. (John 4:24) This is the part that is born-again when one is saved.

The soul is comprised of your mind, will and emotions. This part of you contacts the intellectual world. It involves your feelings and decision making. When the Scriptures mention the soul being saved (James 1:21), it is not talking about forgiveness and going to heaven. Rather, this reference to a soul being saved actually means a change of thinking that conforms to God's ways. This is also referred to as the *renewing of the mind* in the book of Romans. (12:2)

The body is your earth suit. It is simply the house your spirit and soul live in until death. I have often heard the following statement as a way to understand and remember this three-part make up: **"I am a spirit, I have a soul, and I live in a body."**

When a person becomes a new creation in Christ, what exactly becomes new? Your soul? Your body? No, your spirit. If you were 5 feet 10 inches tall before you got saved, you are 5 feet 10 inches tall after you got saved. If you had black hair, you still do. Also, you don't get a new personality when you're born again. If you had wrong thinking beforehand, you still do — except maybe in your understanding of God's forgiveness and love that led you to repentance. Both your body (outside of a physical healing or miracle) and your soul are still the same. However, your spirit is completely brand new. This is outstanding news because your spirit is the most important part. What's more, it's the part that none of us can change on our own; we can make some adjustments to our physical and mental state, but our eternal condition needs an intervention by God Himself.

LIFE STARTS NOW

In the book of Genesis, the very first book in the Bible, we see that God planted a garden and put man in it. (Genesis 2:8) In this garden He put many trees that bore fruit that were good for eating and were to be enjoyed by mankind. There was only one limitation given; there was only one tree from which they were not allowed to eat: the tree of the knowledge of good and evil.

> Then the LORD God took the man and put him in the garden of Eden to tend and keep it. [16] And the LORD God commanded the man, saying, "Of every tree of the garden you may freely eat; [17] but of the tree of the knowledge of good and evil you shall not eat, for in the day that you eat of it you shall surely die." (Genesis 2:15-17)

Notice that God said Adam and Eve would die the day they ate of the tree of the knowledge of good and evil. If you continue reading this whole story, you will find that Adam and Eve both ate of the tree that was forbidden. The question is then, "Did they die?" The answer is absolutely yes!

Adam and Eve did die that day but just not physically. In fact, they both lived for many years after this. That day they died spiritually. The death they experienced meant that they were spiritually separated from God from that time forth.

Unfortunately, people often incorrectly interpret death as being the cessation of existence. They think that when someone dies, they no longer exist. This is never the case for a human being. Therefore, think of death this way: death is separation. When a person dies, their spirit and soul are separated from their body.

Therefore, Adam and Eve didn't stop existing when they died spiritually. They just couldn't connect to God as they previously had. Paul wrote in Romans 5:12, "Therefore, just as through one man [Adam] sin entered the world, and death through sin, and thus death spread to all men, because all sinned—" We need to be re-connected to God; this is why all people today must be born-again.

When we are made new, we are made alive. Our spirits are resurrected from the dead. Christians no longer have the nature of sin and rebellion. Instead, we now have the nature of God. All those who have been made new are now full of love, righteousness, holiness, and so much more!

One of the most important aspects of this new creation business is the part about righteousness. In short, this means that you have *right standing with God*. Whereas you were previously at odds with the Father in heaven because of sin, now you have been made right with Him. You have been justified. A good way to remember what this means is that now it is "just-as-if-I'd" never sinned.

> For He made Him who knew no sin *to be* sin for us, that we might become the righteousness of God in Him. (2 Corinthians 5:21)

Think about it. You are now righteous, not unrighteous. You are now a believer, not an unbeliever. You are saved, not lost. You are a saint instead of a sinner, light and not darkness, accepted and not rejected... We could go on and on. This new position you have with God is absolutely amazing. You can't get any better from a spiritual standpoint. You can't become more saved than you are right now. God will never love you any more or any less.

This righteousness is not in flux from day to day. Although we certainly want to think and act right, failure on our part does not change who we are *in Christ*. No longer think of yourself as an unholy, unworthy, sinful person. See yourself as God sees and has declared you to be.

> Behold what manner of love
> the Father has bestowed on
> us, that we should be called
> children of God! Therefore
> the world does not know us,
> because it did not know Him.
> (1 John 3:1)

Your relationship with God is not limited to just being a believer in Him. You haven't

LIFE STARTS NOW

become religious; you have joined a family. You are His very own child. You are so loved that God calls you one of His own. The next verse goes on to say: "Beloved, now we are children of God; and it has not yet been revealed what we shall be, but we know that when He is revealed, we shall be like Him, for we shall see Him as He is." (I John 3:2) So, becoming God's child is not something that is in the future, it is now. Some day we will fully see that we are like Him, but it is true right now.

Chapter 3
New Habits

Now, let's begin to consider what this new life looks like from day to day. Everything changed spiritually when you were born again, but getting that new spiritual life to have a meaningful impact on your soul and body is going to take some very intentional and consistent action. Salvation is a "one and done" event, but the journey of the Christian life has only just begun when you were saved. You can be a very successful, overcomer-in-life type of Christian or you can struggle year after year with doubt, temptation, and more.

We are not saved by what we do. Neither are we saved by what we don't do. In other words no one goes to heaven because they did so many good works nor because they didn't lie, cheat, or commit adultery. Our behavior simply cannot produce salvation. Look at how it is written in the Bible:

For by grace you have been saved
through faith, and that not of
yourselves; *it is* the gift of God,
[9] not of works, lest anyone should
boast. (Ephesians 2:8-9)

It should be very clear in your mind that you will not go to heaven because you earned it. If you have salvation, you received it as a gift. This is called grace. We have no bragging rights, only thanksgiving to God for all He has given.

However, we were changed inwardly so that we could express outward change. God didn't save us by good works, but He did save us for good works. You will commonly find that man's religious systems get this backward.

For we are His workmanship,
created in Christ Jesus for good
works, which God prepared beforehand that we should walk in
them. (Ephesians 2:10)

We should let our new nature move us to act differently than we did before coming to Christ. In fact, God does want you and me to work His works. We should conduct our lives in a way that honors and glorifies Him. Paul tells us in Ephesians 5:1 that we should "be imitators of God as dear children."

We all have habits. We do certain things over and over again without giving them much thought. Many of these are neither good nor evil. They are just what we have become accustomed to doing. For example, you may get up each morning at a certain time and have a pattern of showering, eating breakfast, and doing other things around the house before heading out to work, school, etc. These habits can be beneficial to kind of automate certain parts of our lives.

Think of what you do on autopilot: maybe some things at work or brushing your teeth and combing your hair a certain way. There are also habits of thinking. We have been trained to think a certain way and so by default follow that pattern whenever certain events take place. For example, some people regularly get angry at other drivers on the road and yell or use *sign language*. Others follow a pattern of fear when hearing about disease or car accidents. You can default to worry and anxiety or even lashing out at others. Whatever your negative thinking patterns are, they can be changed with some time and effort.

Imagine your mind to be like a field that is walked through every day. As a person continually walks the same way, crossing the field in the same pattern day after day, he or she will create a pathway. The grass, weeds, or other plant life will continue to grow everywhere except the path created from continual use. It becomes very easy to get through the field using the path. It is taken daily without any thought. In fact, why would anyone go through the field any other way? This is THE way to get through it. If you decided to create a new route, it would be more work; it would take more time and energy. So, the average person keeps doing the same thing over and over again.

What about your thought patterns? They work the same. By default, you will continue to think the way you have always thought. What if, however, those thoughts run contrary to the Word of God? What if there is a better way to cross the field? Then, it is going to take a quality decision and genuine commitment, accompanied by personal discipline, to start creating a new pathway. It won't feel right at first. It's unfamiliar. You will want to go back to the old way of thinking and if you don't watch out, you will find yourself back on the old trail again. Although, if you will force yourself, day after day, a new pathway will be created in your brain. Soon, it will be as normal as the old one used to be. The old way of thinking will be covered over with new growth, and it will become difficult to go back.

Consider these words from Philippians 4:8: "Finally, brethren, whatever things are true, whatever things *are* noble, whatever things *are* just, whatever things *are* pure, whatever things *are* lovely, whatever things *are* of good report, if *there is* any virtue and if *there*

LIFE STARTS NOW

is anything praiseworthy—meditate on these things." This is a challenge for most people living in a world full of negativity. We have been conditioned to meditate (think) on just the opposite. It is time to make some mental habit changes. It's time to think like God – that is, think His thoughts. This comes from purposefully meditating on His Word.

Romans chapter 12 and verse 2 reads, "And do not be conformed to this world, but be transformed by the renewing of your mind, that you may prove what *is* that good and acceptable and perfect will of God." So, if I am going to break my habits that have been formed by this world, I will need to renew my mind. You can have the righteousness of God in your spirit and still have the mind of a sinner. The will of God, as revealed in His written Word, has the power to create new thought habits. This will make a huge difference in your life going forward. Change your default settings so that you start responding to whatever comes at you in life with God's Word, God's love, and God's wisdom.

> We were buried therefore with
> Him by the baptism into death, so
> that just as Christ was raised from
> the dead by the glorious [power]
> of the Father, so we too might [ha-
> bitually] live *and* behave in newness
> of life. (Romans 6:4 AMPC)

Do you have some bad habits that need to be replaced? How can you habitually live and behave in newness of life? Although there are many good and bad habits we could list, the main thing right now is to create an atmosphere in your life that is conducive to change. The way to do this is to establish a few new habits revolving around this new life you have in Christ. Here are a few:

- Read the Bible daily. (Adopt His thoughts.)
- Pray to the Father throughout your day. (Just talk to Him.)
- Attend a real church each week. (Find a place where God is obvious.)
- Join a small group or serving team. (Develop new connections; these will help tremendously.)

Chapter 4
New Relationships

People influence people. You are a part of this process. You influence and are influenced. This, like many things, can be good or bad. It can bring harm or help. For example, is money good or evil? It is neither, inherently. It can bring many benefits or much destruction. Influence is similar.

Now, let's talk about relationships. Life would be pretty bland without them. They are, in fact, God's idea. He always wanted us to have a relationship with Him and relationships with each other.

I think the point of this chapter should be obvious already. We want to avoid being negatively influenced by those who either don't know or don't love God, and we want to positively influence people around us. Life is a great opportunity, but we can also find ourselves in very real danger.

Consider what happened to Peter and John. After the great miracle of a lame man being healed and the subsequent preaching that drew thousands of people to faith in Jesus, the religious leaders tried to put a stop to this new movement that threatened their doctrine and control over people. After questioning them about the name in which they did these things, Peter answered with great inspiration from the Holy Spirit. Their response was interesting:

> Now when they saw the boldness of Peter and John, and perceived that they were uneducated and un-trained men, they marveled. And they realized that they had been with Jesus. (Acts 4:13)

What did their proximity to Jesus have to do with anything? Well, Jesus was very bold. He taught with great authority: "And they were astonished at His teaching, for He taught them as one having authority, and not as the scribes." (Mark 1:22) He commanded unclean spirits to come out and they did:

"Then they were all amazed and spoke among themselves, saying, "What a word this *is*! For with authority and power He commands the unclean spirits, and they come out." (Luke 4:36) Jesus was not intimidated by the religious leaders or the devil. Now, these guys were acting just like Him. They were carrying the same attitude and speaking with the same power that Jesus did.

Here is the point: **we become like those with whom we spend a lot of time.** We have all picked up little phrases and colloquialisms from friends and family without trying to mimic them. Knowing this, a wise person will monitor very closely those who are allowed to speak into his life.

> Do not be deceived: "Evil company corrupts good habits."
> (1 Corinthians 15:33)

I've heard some respond to statements like this by saying, "I'm not affected by the people around me like others are." Really? Maybe you are but don't realize it. There is a reason for this verse being included in the

Bible. It is because of the tendency for people to exempt themselves by thinking their associations don't really matter and that they don't need to make any changes in this area of life. When you see a scripture verse start with "Do not be deceived," take note. You might be tempted to discard what is coming next but don't. Do not be deceived!

Maybe you are already thinking of your current associations. Are you more likely to drink and use drugs when you are around certain people? Do you join in with the gossip of others? Do some people discourage you from going to church – maybe overtly or maybe just by planning events every Sunday? Who in your life inspires you to live for God and become more committed, more loving, and hungrier for spiritual things? Are you thinking, "I influence my friends positively more than they influence me negatively?" Great! But, really? Okay. Just checking.

Here is another verse along these lines: "He who walks with wise *men* will be wise, but the companion of fools will be destroyed."

LIFE STARTS NOW

(Proverbs 13:20) Hmm. That's a good reason to pay attention to this chapter. I have wanted so much to help certain people to succeed in life but knew it would never happen until they got around a new crowd.

Maybe all your relationships are currently with very positive, God-loving people who helped you to come to Jesus. Maybe you were the only one in your circle of friends and family that was holding out, or maybe you are the first among those you hang with to get saved. Perhaps you fall somewhere in the middle. No matter which description fits you the best, I want to share about a new company. No, not a business plan to sign up for, but a group of people with whom you "do" life.

Peter and John, after bringing healing to the lame man and then preaching to those who had seen the miracle, were hauled before the chief priests and elders. They demanded that the disciples not speak or teach in the name of Jesus anymore. What was Peter and John's reaction? The first thing they did was to go to their own company.

34

And being let go, they went
to their own company, and re-
ported all that the chief priests
and elders had said unto them.
(Acts 4:23 KJV)

Their own company was their new spiritual family. You have one too. When you got saved, you joined a family. It is usually called the Church or the Body of Christ.

You need to know that God's design is that we should spend time together. Here is the way it was written in the book of Hebrews: "And let us consider how we may spur one another on toward love and good deeds, 25 not giving up meeting together, as some are in the habit of doing, but encouraging one another—and all the more as you see the Day approaching." (Hebrews 10:24-25)

We are to get together for worship, prayer, teaching, service, giving, and more. We are to support one another through fellowship and comradery. We are much stronger together than we will ever be on our own.

LIFE STARTS NOW

For if they fall, one will lift up his companion. But woe to him *who is* alone when he falls, For *he has* no one to help him up. (Ecclesiastes 4:10)

Take advantage of this new family you have. We still have our own issues we are working on. We are all still learning and growing. However, you are better off with us, and we are better off with you. The temptation will come to isolate yourself from other believers but don't because you will be more vulnerable to spiritual attack. Resist the temptation. Proverbs 18:1 reads, "A man who isolates himself seeks his own desire; He rages against all wise judgment." Don't be self-seeking. Don't rage against wise judgment. Instead of isolating yourself, go hang out with fellow Christians and church family members. You need them, and they need you.

It's not that you must cut off all of your previous relationships. They need you now more than ever. You have more to offer. You are connected to the God of the universe. In fact, He is your Dad! Tell them what happened to you. They might follow you into salvation right away. If not, be patient with them. Maybe it took you a while to come to faith in Jesus too. If some people are attacking you for being a Christian or just really pulling you down, it may be wise to put some space between them and you for a time until you can grow spiritually and not be hindered by their unbelief. Then, you can reengage with more strength and wisdom so that God can use you to minister salvation to them.

Making new friends often takes a little effort. Get out of your comfort zone. Go to church. Initiate a conversation. Sign up for a small group. Find out what is happening for people your age to make it easier for connections. Pray, asking God to connect you with the right people. Many of us have relationships with certain people that we are totally convinced were ordained by God. You will have these too.

Chapter 5
New Way of Living

As you therefore have received
Christ Jesus the Lord, so walk in
Him. (Colossians 2:6)

You are a new creation in Christ. You
have a new Father—God Himself. You have
a new spiritual family. Much has changed.
It all happened in a moment of time when
you put your faith in Jesus as your Savior.
Now, let's think about how this new life
works. What are the old ways of doing it
versus the new ways? If you were to move
to a new country, there would be laws and
customs to learn related to things like driving and taxes. You would have a hard time
if you didn't learn and follow those laws
and customs. Now, you are a part of the
kingdom of God, and there are laws that
govern it. It's time to begin renewing your
mind by learning the rules and principles of

God's Kingdom in order to avoid *driving on the wrong side of the road.*

> Do not be conformed to this world, but be transformed by the renewing of your mind, that you may prove what *is* that good and acceptable and perfect will of God. (Romans 12:2)

Although there is a lifetime of learning ahead, there are a couple of basics that can help get you started. As stated above in Colossians 2:6, you are to walk in Christ the same way you received Him. This is very simple yet powerful. You received forgiveness of sin by faith in what Jesus did through His death and resurrection. You didn't earn it, deserve, or work for it in any way. You simply received the gift by faith. God's part in this equation is called grace; your part is called faith. You likely got saved before you were faithful to church, gave your tithe, had a consistent prayer life, or did much else for God. In this same way, you can receive anything else you need. Healing for the body, deliverance from addictions, and answers to prayer will come because of God's grace and your choice to believe in it.

> For in it the righteousness of God is revealed from faith to faith; as it is written, "The just shall live by faith." (Romans 1:17)

The phrase "the just shall live by faith" is found four times in the Bible. It is not an isolated concept but a governing principle by which all Christians are to live. The "just" mentioned here are those who have been made righteous by putting their faith in Jesus. The living by faith part is what you do. The contrast would be living by sight—living by your senses. 2 Corinthians 5:7 reads, "For we walk by faith, not by sight." Walking by sight is the opposite of walking by faith.

This new way of living has to do with your choice of believing what God has said over what you see and feel. If you feel like a bad person – maybe unsaved, unaccepted, or unloved – choose to believe what God has already said about your life:

You are saved.
> If you confess with your
> mouth the Lord Jesus and
> believe in your heart that
> God has raised Him from
> the dead, you will be saved.
> (Romans 10:9)

You are accepted.
> To the praise of the glory
> of His grace, by which He
> made us accepted in the
> Beloved. (Ephesians 1:6)

You are loved.
> But God demonstrates His
> own love toward us, in that
> while we were still sinners,
> Christ died for us.
> (Romans 5:8)

If you live by what you see and feel, your life will be a constant roller coaster. You will be up one day and down the next. If, however, you learn to live by faith, you can live a steady and consistent life because God's Word never changes.

When dealing with sickness, disease or injuries, for example, you have a choice to make. Do you just accept this condition as you have in the past, or do you apply God's promises to your situation? You can decide to take God at His word, using verses like these:

> [1]Bless the Lord, O my soul; And all that is within me, *bless* His holy name!
> [2]Bless the Lord, O my soul, And forget not all His benefits:
> [3]Who forgives all your iniquities, Who heals all your diseases.
> (Psalms 103:1-3)

> That it might be fulfilled which was spoken by Isaiah the prophet, saying: "He Himself took our infirmities And bore *our* sicknesses." (Matthew 8:17)

> Who Himself bore our sins in His own body on the tree, that we, having died to sins, might live for righteousness—by whose stripes you were healed. (1 Peter 2:24)

Living by sight says that these verses can't be true when pain and other symptoms exist. Living by faith denies the right of those physical problems to remain. Choose today to live by faith for your health and healing.

Likewise, when it comes to financial needs, you can say, "I'm broke, I don't have enough to live or to give," or you can say, "My God supplies all my need." (Philippians 4:19) You can declare that money, jobs, and opportunities are coming your way because of God's blessing on your life. Choose today to live by faith for your provision and financial well being.

You see, Christians deal with much of the same things as everyone else. What's the difference then? Christians just think differently. Our faith in God's Word makes us talk like everything is going to be okay; our faith causes us to agree with God's promises. We pray with great boldness and confidence that our Father, Who loves us, both hears and gives us what we ask:

LIFE STARTS NOW

Now this is the confidence that
we have in Him, that if we ask
anything according to His will, He
hears us. [15] And if we know that
He hears us, whatever we ask, we
know that we have the petitions
that we have asked of Him.
(1 John 5:14-15)

The old way of life is full of worry, anxiety,
and fear. In it, we often would dwell on the
"what ifs." "What if my car breaks down."
"What if I lose my job." "What if I get
cancer." "What if I get into a car accident."
"What if my child gets hooked on drugs."
There are a thousand negative things that can
occupy our minds each day. Again, that's the
old life. In this new life we pray instead. No,
we don't just speak our worries and fears out
loud to God; we ask Him to change things.
We continually give thanks to Him until we
see bad things leave. Paul said it this way in
Philippians:

Be anxious for nothing, but in
everything by prayer and suppli-

cation, with thanksgiving, let your
requests be made known to God;
[7] and the peace of God, which sur-
passes all understanding, will guard
your hearts and minds through
Christ Jesus.
(Philippians 4:6-7)

This is so much better. Don't worry, pray.
The peace of God will fill you. People who
knew you before may wonder why you aren't
so stressed out anymore. This life is awe-
some!

When you pray, here is the approach. Ask
the Father in the name of Jesus. It's not that
your words need to be scripted or perfectly
stated, but Jesus said we should pray this
way. Read these verses to understand what
Jesus said:

You did not choose Me, but I chose
you and appointed you that you
should go and bear fruit, and *that*
your fruit should remain, that <u>what-
ever you ask the Father in My name
He may give you</u>. (John 15:16)

LIFE STARTS NOW

And in that day you will ask Me
nothing. Most assuredly, I say to
you, whatever you ask the Father
in My name He will give you.
(John 16:23)

Of course, there are many more verses that
deal with the subject of faith and prayer that
you will learn as you establish the new habits
taught in chapter three. For now, begin to
train yourself to look to the Word when life
throws you a curve ball; Scripture will then
become the basis for your faith. Secondly, tell
your Heavenly Father what you are believing
for. Refuse to worry and speak negatively
about anything. Ask and then give thanks
continually that the Father has both heard
and answered your prayer.

Chapter 6
What's Next?

A logical question now would be, "What's next—are there any steps I should take immediately that would help me to grow in Christ?" Absolutely yes! In addition to putting into practice the principles laid out in this book, which is a continual process, I recommend two baptisms. You might be thinking, "What? Two? Is this a typo?" It's not. Let be briefly explain what these two baptisms are.

Baptism in Water

The scriptures lay out very clearly that the believing person should be baptized in water. The word baptize simply means to immerse or submerge. So, when a person is water baptized, they briefly go completely underwater. Here is the way it is written in Acts 8:37-38:

> Then Philip said, "If you believe with all your heart, you may." And

he answered and said, "I believe
that Jesus Christ is the Son of
God." [38] So he commanded the
chariot to stand still. And both
Philip and the eunuch went down
into the water, and he baptized him.

Some who are reading this book may have
had an experience prior to salvation of being
baptized. In fact, I have had people who
received the Lord in our church services tell
me that they had attended a different church
for years and had been baptized in water.
Then, after attending our services and hearing, as a part of the Gospel, that they must be
born again, they got saved. Think about that,
they got baptized without being saved first.
This is backward. The question then is about
whether or not they should be baptized again.
The answer is yes.

Notice in the above scripture that the
eunuch first said, "I believe that Jesus Christ
is the Son of God." (v. 37) Only then did
Phillip agree to baptize him. So, being baptized before salvation doesn't mean much. It
is a non-event. Your new life began when you

accepted Jesus. Remember old things have passed away. (2 Corinthians 5:17) Anything the "old guy" did is dead and gone.

One of the first things Jesus told his disciples to do after He left the earth was to make disciples of all nations. The interesting part of this commandment is that the very first step in this process is baptism.

> Go therefore and make disciples
> of all the nations, baptizing them
> in the name of the Father and of
> the Son and of the Holy Spirit.
> (Matthew 28:19)

So, a person can't truly be a disciple of Jesus until they are baptized. Let me make a distinction here. You can be saved without water baptism, but becoming a disciple (a disciplined follower of Jesus) requires this vital step.

This might raise another valid question: what is so important about going under the water? Well, it's obviously not about the water. You can go in as a dry sinner and come out as a wet sinner. You can go in as a dry Christian and come out no different than you went in except the fact that you are now waterlogged. Also, it is not about religion. God does not instruct us to do things that have no value to living out our new life in Christ. Water baptism is all about what it represents and what we believe when we participate. When there is an understanding of what Jesus did for us and how baptism symbolizes it, there is a powerful effect upon our souls (mind, will, and emotions).

Peter wrote about baptism and related it to Noah and his family being saved from the great flood in the ark. (Read Genesis 6:13-8:14 for original account of Noah.)

> And baptism, which is a figure [of their deliverance], does now also save you [from inward questionings and fears], not by the removing of outward body filth [bathing], but by [providing you with] the answer of a good and clear conscience (inward cleanness and peace) before God [because you are demonstrating what you

believe to be yours] through the resurrection of Jesus Christ.
(1 Peter 3:21 AMPC)

Just like Noah and his family were not saved by the water but rather by the ark, we are not saved by baptism waters but by faith in the death, burial, and resurrection of Jesus. Baptism is an outward act that shows in a physical way that you died with Christ and were raised together with Him to new life. This act is both a testimony to others of your faith in Jesus and a declaration that you can benefit from personally. It is you shouting out loud to all who will witness it that your old man is dead and you are now risen with Christ. This demonstration when performed by faith in what Jesus did will have a deep and lasting impact on your own life. Again, it doesn't give you eternal life, but it certainly helps you to know that it's yours so that you can live free.

Many people have experienced healing, freedom from addictions, deliverance from sinful habits, and other blessings from God during their baptisms. Others enjoy an overwhelming sense of joy or peace in God's presence. It really is a God-ordained activity that He personally gets involved in with us. This is something new believers should do as soon as possible.

Baptism in the Holy Spirit

First of all, the idea of being baptized in the Spirit has its origins in the Old Testament. The prophet Joel long ago told of a day when God's Spirit would be poured out. You can find this passage of scripture in the book named after this prophet of God:

> And it shall come to pass afterward
> That I will pour out My Spirit on all flesh;
> Your sons and your daughters shall prophesy,
> Your old men shall dream dreams,
> Your young men shall see visions.
> [29] And also on *My* menservants and on *My* maidservants
> I will pour out My Spirit in those days.
> (Joel 2:28-29)

Secondly, waiting for this promise to be fulfilled was the last command that Jesus gave His disciples, the first believers, before He left earth. So, it must be pretty important for each and every believer to receive this promise as well:

> And being assembled together with *them*, He commanded them not to depart from Jerusalem, but to wait for the Promise of the Father, "which," *He said*, "you have heard from Me; 5 for John truly baptized with water, but you shall be baptized with the Holy Spirit not many days from now."
> (Acts 1:4-5)

Jesus didn't want them to try living their new lives and doing what He had commanded them to do without this empowerment. It's kind of like if you were to go on a road trip: one of the first things you would do is fill up your gas tank. Why? You want to make it to your destination. Now, notice the following verse:

LIFE STARTS NOW

> But you shall receive power when
> the Holy Spirit has come upon
> you; and you shall be witnesses to
> Me in Jerusalem, and in all Judea
> and Samaria, and to the end of the
> earth. (Acts 1:8)

So, for the disciples to do what Jesus said to do, they would need this power of the Holy Spirit. (If they needed the power then, we need it today.) About 120 people waited in the upper room of where they were staying (Acts 1:14). Then...

> [1]When the Day of Pentecost had
> fully come, they were all with one
> accord in one place. [2] And sudden-
> ly there came a sound from heav-
> en, as of a rushing mighty wind,
> and it filled the whole house where
> they were sitting. [3] Then there
> appeared to them divided tongues,
> as of fire, and *one* sat upon each
> of them. [4] And they were all filled
> with the Holy Spirit and began to
> speak with other tongues, as the
> Spirit gave them utterance.
> (Acts 2:1-4)

Let me draw your attention to the fact that when those believers gathered in the Upper Room and were filled with the Holy Spirit, they were given the ability to speak in *other tongues*. (Tongues is just another way to say *languages*.) When the believers, who were now filled with the Spirit and speaking in tongues, busted out of the Upper Room, those who were in the streets "heard" them speaking in their native languages. What were the believers saying? They were testifying of the mighty works of God:

> [6]And there were dwelling in Jerusalem Jews, devout men, from every nation under heaven. And when this sound occurred, the multitude came together, and were confused, because everyone heard them speak in his own language. [7]Then they were all amazed and marveled, saying to one another, "Look, are not all these who speak Galileans? [8]And how *is it that* we hear, each in our own language in which we were born? [9]Parthians and Medes and Elamites, those

LIFE STARTS NOW

dwelling in Mesopotamia, Judea and Cappadocia, Pontus and Asia, [10] Phrygia and Pamphylia, Egypt and the parts of Libya adjoining Cyrene, visitors from Rome, both Jews and proselytes, [11] Cretans and Arabs—we hear them speaking in our own tongues the wonderful works of God."

In the first infilling seen in Acts 2, the people were given languages not known or understood by them. The same is true today. When a person speaks in tongues from the Holy Spirit, it comes straight out of their spirit and bypasses their mind. Paul said it this way:

> For he who speaks in a tongue does not speak to men but to God, for no one understands *him*; however, in the spirit he speaks mysteries. (1 Corinthians 14:2)

> For if I pray in a tongue, my spirit prays, but my understanding is unfruitful. (1 Corinthians 14:14)

Lastly, although the disciples and other believers had to wait for the gift of the Holy Spirit, we do not. We can now receive at any time after salvation! I am encouraging you as a new believer to not wait. Go ahead and receive now! You need His power in order to live your best Christian life and to fulfill all that He has for you to do.

α

How to Receive the Holy Spirit

Just like other gifts of God, receiving the Holy Spirit is easy because it is done by faith. You can simply ask, receive, and begin speaking in other tongues. Read what Jesus said about it:

> "So I say to you, ask, and it will be given to you; seek, and you will find; knock, and it will be opened to you. [10] For everyone who asks receives, and he who seeks finds, and to him who knocks it will be opened. [11] If a son asks for bread from any father among you, will he

LIFE STARTS NOW

give him a stone? Or if *he asks* for
a fish, will he give him a serpent
instead of a fish? [12] Or if he asks
for an egg, will he offer him a
scorpion? [13] If you then, being evil,
know how to give good gifts to
your children, how much more will
your heavenly Father give the Holy
Spirit to those who ask Him!"
(Luke 11:9-13)

Would you like someone to help by pray-
ing with you? Contact the leaders in your new
church. Tell them you want to receive the
baptism in the Holy Spirit. If they don't know
what to do, you are in the wrong church.

You can certainly go to your Father in
heaven directly. He hears and will respond to
you. Pray a prayer like this:

> Father, according to Jesus, I will
> receive power when the Holy
> Spirit comes upon me. He also
> said that you would give me the
> Holy Spirit if I ask and that ev-
> eryone who asks receives. So I

58

ask now for the gift of the Holy Spirit. Baptize me; fill me to overflowing. I receive Him now, in Jesus' name. Amen.

Now, open your mouth and begin to speak out the words that He gives you. Keep speaking. Let it flow! Do this every day. It will benefit you greatly.

Conclusion

This is the beginning of a great adventure, and your future in God is great. He has a wonderful plan for your life. In difficult times, always run to Him and not away from Him. He will be your help in time of need. He will be your strength and give you the wisdom to navigate the rest of your days on earth. Keep learning, growing, and walking closely with the Lord. Your new life has begun!

Glossary
Common Christian Words

As you begin your relationship with God, you may come to realize that Christians have their own "language." There are many words and phrases that you may not know and/or be accustomed to using that you will hear in church and conversation with other believers. Many of them are taken directly out of the Bible. Here are several:

Bible – A collection of 66 books that were written by 40 authors, who were inspired by God over a period of about 1600 years. It is commonly called the Word, God's Word, or the Scriptures.

Old Testament – The first 39 books of the Bible (Genesis through Malachi) that contain a history of certain events prior to the coming of Jesus Christ.

New Testament – The last 27 books of the Bible (Matthew through Revelation) that begin with the life of Jesus and mostly contain instruction for Christians today.

LIFE STARTS NOW

<u>Gospel</u> – Literally, it means "good news." It is the message that Jesus suffered and died for the sins of mankind and was then raised from the dead, providing forgiveness and eternal life to all who believe.

<u>Conviction</u> – An awareness of or a belief in something that God is saying to a person.

<u>Faith</u> – Persuasion; an overall set of beliefs (e.g. the Christian faith); a specific conviction of something God has promised.

<u>Redeem</u> – To buy back. This was what Jesus did for us on the cross; He purchased our salvation.

<u>Righteousness</u> – Being made right with God; justified.

<u>Saints </u> – All members of God's family; those who have been born-again by putting their faith in Jesus as the sacrifice for their sins and victor over death.

<u>Grace</u> – The unearned ability and favor of God toward mankind, enabling him to be and do what would be impossible without it. Every

gift or ability from God comes by His grace.

<u>Sanctify</u> – To set apart or make holy.

<u>Trinity</u> – A word used to describe the three-fold nature of God. He is three persons: Father, Son (Jesus), and Holy Spirit.

<u>Church</u> – A gathering of believers for the purpose of worship, teaching, serving, and spreading the gospel.

<u>Pastor</u> – An individual that God gifts to lead a local church.

<u>Apostle</u> – One who is sent by God to do a particular work like starting new churches or preaching to a certain group of people.

<u>Paul</u> – An apostle in the early church who wrote many New Testament books.

<u>Worship</u> – Living life for God. It is often used to define singing and speaking words of praise and thanksgiving to the Lord.

<u>Tithe</u> – 10% of a person's income that is given to God through the church to carry out ministry.

LIFE STARTS NOW

<u>Presence of God</u> – This simply refers to God being here but is often used referencing some tangibility or awareness of Him.

<u>Move of the Spirit</u> – The activities of the Holy Spirit (Holy Ghost; God) in the lives of individuals or the church. It can include salvations, healings, prophecies, etc.

<u>Laying on of Hands</u> – The placing of one person's hands on the physical body of another for the purpose of healing or transferring other blessings. It often accompanies prayer.

<u>Tongues</u> – Languages given by the Holy Spirit to individuals that are not known by the person speaking or typically by those listening.

Made in the USA
Columbia, SC
08 December 2023

28057117R00037